Notes on Nothing

"My old friend went into his garden one day and had an experience of nothing. Of being nothing in the midst of everything. Of realising that everything is also nothing. Sometimes I feel I have this non-experience when I'm writing. Maybe you have had it doing whatever you do, or don't do, or just while sitting in a garden... It's a very hard thing to put into words: impossible, actually. But sometimes poets and musicians and wise souls gesture towards it, beautifully. That's what my old friend has done here. Give your self the slip for an hour. Read this book."

— Zadie Smith, author of *White Teeth* and *The Fraud*

"Like a saner P.K. Dick undergoing a gentler VALIS-type experience, the author offers insights on the weeks in which he ceased to be. This eloquent, sparse and wise book nudges readers sideways into the calm revelation of emptiness."

— John Tresch, Professor of History of Art and Science, The Warburg Institute, and author of *The Reason for the Darkness of the Night: Edgar Allan Poe and the Forging of American Science*

"To the question of why is there something rather than nothing, the author's response is that there isn't. And since there is nothing rather than something, he has nothing to persuade us of, nor any prescription to offer us either. That in itself comes as a relief. What's shared instead in this beautiful book is an experience its author has had, and so which we might have too. There's no map to this experience, which is the experience of nothing after all, but even to read of it is to feel one's sense of self and world exerting a little less pressure and getting subtly rearranged."

— Devorah Baum, writer and filmmaker, author of *On Marriage*

"This small gem of a book straddles the ego's dilemma of falling into and then out of a deep enlightenment experience. It is a normal and natural struggle to vividly remember and make sense of such an experience, even though it is inclined to vanish in its own emptiness. As this captivating memoir reminds us of our true nature, it should be placed among the spiritual classics. Both inspired and inspiring, *Notes on Nothing* is a must-read for all those interested in exploring the miracle of consciousness."

— Michael Gellert, Jungian analyst, Zen practitioner, and author of *The Way of the Small: Why Less Is Truly More* and *Legacy of Darkness and Light*

"It is difficult to find words to describe what happens when our sense of a separate self dissolves – because, as the author discovered in his garden, nothing happens. Here he has reached beyond the silence to craft an eloquent, personal-yet-nonpersonal testament to the true nature we all share. His account is all the more affecting as it unfolds within ordinary family life, and affirms its value. The truth he uncovers – beautiful and poignant in equal measure – leaves us with precisely nothing to do, except feel its light shine."

— Clare Carlisle, Professor of Philosophy, King's College London, and author of *Spinoza's Religion* and *Philosopher of the Heart: The Restless Life of Søren Kierkegaard*

NOTES ON NOTHING

The Joy Of Being Nobody

by Anonymous

AS IS PRESS

PO Box: 39A31
3370 Glendale Blvd.
Los Angeles, CA 90039
www.as-is.press

Copyright © As Is Press 2024
All rights reserved

Designed by C.C. Day

Printed Sheridan Books in the United States of America

ISBN: 979-8-9907154-0-0

Library of Congress Cataloging-in-Publication data is on
file with the publisher

CONTENTS

FOREWORD

This is a book about Nothing. You could also say it's a book about Everything. Most accurately perhaps, it's a book about *Nothing-as-Everything* and *Everything-as-Nothing*.

It takes as its spine an account of a specific experience that seemed to happen to me, during which there wasn't very much "Me" around. There have been many names given to these kinds of "non-experiences", depending on what tradition or viewpoint they are being seen from.

Here let's call it *a meeting with Nothing, that never actually happened.*

This book is meant to be read by those who may identify as "spiritual seekers", those who would never dream of doing so, and everyone in between. These pages make no such distinctions. I have tried to write as much as possible from direct experience, and to avoid using other people's frameworks or phrases. So you won't find explicit references to things like "Advaita Vedanta" or "Zen" or "non-duality" and so on.

That said, many of the words I use echo those often used by others who have apparently had similar non-experiences to mine. I say more about this in the acknowledgements section at the end.

———

I've chosen not to use my name on the cover of this book. This is because who I am does not really matter. The story of me is only a story - it's no more and no less important or ordinary than that. These pages don't seek to teach anything. They don't prescribe anything. I don't claim here to be any kind of "expert" or "guide" or even to be *credible* on these matters.

If this can be my story, it could be anyone's. It could be yours.

You might call this account only a *suggestion of a possibility*. A kind of report from Nothing, written as evocatively as this writer is able. Some readers might find these words frustrating, or irritating, or even nonsensical. Others might find that the words resonate. They might find with one reading or repeated readings that there can be an *inducement* of something in the words, beyond the attempt to intellectually understand them.

If you choose to read these pages as a work of fiction, or an imaginative projection, or "thought experiment", that's also fine.

Either way, take heart, dear friend: Nothing is really gained or lost.

Interspersed through the text that follows is a sequence of poems that I wrote during the period of non-experience described here. I have reproduced them more-or-less unedited from that time, in order to try to better convey the spirit in which they were written. A particular poem should not at all be seen as an *illustration* of a point. In fact it may be the other way round; perhaps the point seeks to illustrate the poem.

INTRODUCTION

It was initially not my intention to write about Nothing. It didn't feel like something that was *necessary* for me to do. In fact, it's ultimately not even something that is *possible* to do. But perhaps because this Someone is a writer, and has been now for close to twenty-five years, at a certain point writing this just seemed to spontaneously want to happen.

That seemingly autonomous impulse hit me in the early hours one July morning, in London. My family and I were spending a couple of months back in our homeland, England. During the last week of our stay, we house-sat for old friends, in the northeast of the city.

Our friends have a beautiful cat named Pippi. She's a grey-white Siberian, long-haired, ear-tufted, with lucent blue eyes. She's also hypoallergenic, which made her safe for my wife, T., and our eldest daughter to be around; they are both quite seriously allergic to cats.

Now, I should say that I have an unexpected history of connection with cats. "Unexpected" because I wouldn't characterize myself as especially connected to animals in general, at least no more than most people. But I seem to have always had a thing about cats. Since I was a child, I have spontaneously drawn images of cat people, amalgams of cats and humans, often dressed in suits and walking city streets. Many times I have encountered in dreams and journeys a big cat spirit - a jaguar or puma - and relate to this spirit as a guardian and guide. There's a larger story there to unpack I'm sure, but suffice to say, for reasons unknown to me, cats have appeared at several meaningful moments in my life.

The first night we stayed at our friends' house, Pippi jumped onto the mattress in the darkness and curled up with us in the corner of the bed. I turned off the lamp and, the sound of Pippi's purring rising in the shadows, fell asleep.

I woke at 4am. Some time in the night Pippi had moved over to me, and was now lying prone, fully stretched out along the side of my right leg. I was pinned by her warm, soft weight. She was fast asleep, and was pretty much unmovable when I tried to shift position. I'd been rudely woken, but despite a certain feeling of frustration I couldn't muster much anger at Pippi. All I managed was an involuntary laugh, dancing out of me into the stillness of the blue, quiet room.

At that moment I knew that I was going to write these pages. The thought of them had not remotely existed in my head, and then suddenly there it was. Lying on my back next to my sleeping wife, pinned by a sleeping cat, I started drafting sentences in my head, unable to stop myself, or to slip back to sleep again for several more hours.

Above all the other notions that chattered away in my mind that night, my strongest sense was that what mattered was to try to find a *personal way to approach the impersonal*, as paradoxical as that was.

Perhaps I could take my own "non-experience" from several months before, and with it gesture at Nothing as it were from different angles, lighting up one (non-existent) aspect and then another, like a many-faceted jewel being turned under a lamp.

What follows is my attempt to turn Nothing in the light like a jewel.

It will be a failed attempt, because Nothing can never be spoken about.

In the end there is nothing to be said.

———

Thank you for your kind assistance, Pippi.

———

In November of 2022 I had an experience of Nothingness. A better thing to call it is a *non-experience*, because it amounted to an apparent dissolving or a thinning-out of the sense of a separate individual who might "experience" something. This non-experience lasted about two weeks. After that, "experience" seemed to return, or, you could say, *Nothing was apparently replaced with Everything again.*

I think it's likely that most human beings have had this gap or "non-experience" appear in their lives at some point, if only for a passing moment. *Nothing* may become suddenly and unavoidably evident while out on a walk, or in a quiet moment alone, or even amongst a crowd of strangers. It may become evident like the jarring impact of a physical shock, or the flicker of light against a wall, or a ripple spreading out across the surface of a lake.

Sometimes we can spend our lives longing for this briefly felt lacuna of Nothing to return to us, to engulf us again, admitting us for good into its openness, its stillness, its peace, its rest.

These pages will explore the suggestion that the revelation is that this longing for Nothing is the *exact trick* of the illusion of being a separate Someone.

Because everything is, and always has been, *already* Nothing.

Nothing is all there ever was, is, or will be - even the longing for Nothing.

It's not really clear to me what led to the two-week period of non-experience, in terms of causal events in time. There's a *story* I can tell about it. But I honestly can't say with conviction or certainty that anything I ever did *caused* this non-experience to happen - or "not-happen". (And after all, from the point of view of Nothing, there *is no causation at all*, which may be why it seems unconvincing to talk about it.)

It's certainly part of the story that I had been involved in a healing ceremony with a friend of mine, just before the period of non-experience began. My friend has many years' professional experience as a practitioner of traditional Shamanic healing, and we have worked together several times in the past. She was kind enough to lead an online ceremony for the two of us, in which she helped disentangle the beloved but somewhat troublesome figure of my Indian grandmother from my psyche. Uma B. - my father's mother - is her own story, one that will have to be told elsewhere. It's enough to say here that whatever exactly occurred during the ceremony, my experience of it was powerful, and by the end of it I was exhausted. I went to bed that night feeling heavy and nauseous, and dreamed very intensely.

The next morning, I felt good. There was a sense of peace, and of relief, in my body. I had breakfast with T. and my daughters. When they left for school, I went as usual into my office at the back of the house.

I tried to work, staring blankly at the computer screen. But I just couldn't concentrate. There was no impulse whatsoever inside me to write, or even to *think* about writing. I finally gave up, taking off my glasses and kneading my temples.

It was a warm day (the weather where I live is dappled and beautiful in November, in contrast to the grey winter squalls of my London childhood), so I walked out into the garden. T. has spent several years curating, planting, and maintaining a wonderland of native plants which bloom all the way up the little hill at the back of the house. Cacti, agaves, succulents; rustling greens and smooth dusty blues and vivid orange-and-white flowers which explode all through the spring.

I walked slowly up through this labyrinth of plants to the top of the hill. I sat down on a chair under the crude arbor we've built up there out of railway sidings. I stared down into the planting below me. A particular desert broom bush seemed to expand to fill my field of vision. A dense, almost impossibly complex tangle of branching green stems formed a net of shadow, through which little white butterflies and crane flies occasionally flitted, catching sunlight.

My body was abruptly filled with a deep stillness, as if my whole nervous system had suddenly relaxed, much more deeply than I was used to. I had a sense of dissolving, of spreading outwards. The boundaries not just of my body but of my *selfhood* seemed to be thinning out and then merging with the garden, and the leaf-shadowed morning.

No time. No boundaries in space.

All that was left was just *Life*.

It was seen very clearly that there was nothing and no one.

No one was here. Nothing was happening.

"Life" - *This* - was Nothing. Nothing, happening. Nothing, appearing as Everything.

Not "nothing" in the sense of an absence, a lack of "something". But Nothing in the sense of No-thing. No-thing that was *separate* from any-thing else.

No-thing that *knew*, because there was no-thing outside itself *to be known*, no-thing that *experienced*, because there was no-thing outside itself *to experience*, no-thing that could or would ever really *be*.

And it was seen that not only was there Nothing, but there had *always* been Nothing.

No one was *ever* here. Nothing had *ever* happened.

Just this: without time, without space, without end, and without beginning.

I sat there for almost three hours, hardly moving my body. Occasionally I would run my heels in two slowly deepening troughs along the ground.

My mind seemed to be racing on and on, round and round. It was trying to process what felt like a thousand competing impressions and questions, in the face of what suddenly seemed so obviously evident. But my *body* remained extremely still and relaxed. It was as if my nervous system had released a tension that it had probably held onto since I was an infant. The simple tension of feeling like *Something*, like *Someone*.

One of the questions my mind was urgently trying to process was: *What is it that's processing all this, when there's only Nothing here?*

I couldn't yet come to an answer to this question, or to the others that churned in my mind, a whirligig of thoughts, spinning and spinning.

———

Eventually I walked down off the hill and went inside. The deep sense of stillness and relaxation in my body hadn't gone away. There was a feeling that although things were seemingly happening, nothing in particular *needed* to happen. I would say these two qualities were the underlying constant of the whole period - they did not lessen in any discernible way until the apparent end of it.

T. was home, and I said something to her about having just had a "crazy experience" out in the garden. I count myself extraordinarily lucky that T. is my life partner in many different senses and on many different levels, and has been for more than twenty years now. She is not easily surprised by whatever strange dish I might bring to her table. I think that during those first days of the non-experience, she guessed that some apparent "shift" had seemingly happened in me. But I wasn't able to speak to her about what was really going on (or not going on) for quite some time. It seemed too much. It seemed *un*speakable:

There is no me. There is no you.

There has never been me. There has never been you.

This is really, really the case, my love. Evident, clear, unavoidable.

How could I express this conviction, earnestly, with the sense of obviousness that I felt at that moment, to her?

Frankly, my concern was that she would be *worried* for me. That I would become alienated from her. That I would *lose* her. So I didn't speak in detail to T. about what had apparently become of me.

There was more that had to unfold before I could do that.

———

The sense of a separate person burns away. What is left is Nothing.

The jewel turns, and Nothing is—

Life.

Turns again, and there is—

Formlessness.

This.

Boundlessness.

Unknown.

Emptiness.

Absolute wholeness.

Freedom.

Every one of these names is useless.

The jewel does not exist.

———

When the sense of a separate person thins, there is a sort of paradoxical double-sensing.

There is wonder. An amazed, awe-struck joy, constantly on the verge of laughter that wants to convulse itself up in the chest and set the shoulders rolling. *How absurd and hilarious, to be Nothing!* For Everything to *always* have been Nothing! How completely nonsensically stupid it is, how ridiculous!

But at the same time, it is a *calm* joy. A paradoxically *ordinary* wonder. What had happened on the hill was gentle, matter-of-fact - in a sense, innocuous.

Nothingness is completely ordinary.

There is no Mind-Blowing Ecstasy. No Big Bang. No Transcendent Experience. No Spectacular Awakening.

It is the *end of the need* for a Big Bang, for a Transcendent Experience, for a Spectacular Awakening.

It is the *end of the possibility* for a Big Bang, for a Transcendent Experience, for a Spectacular Awakening.

It is the *end of need*. It is the *end of possibility*.

Because what could Nothing ever need?

What could Nothing ever do?

What could be more ordinary than Life itself?

———

What is it that's processing all this, when there's only Nothing here? The beginning of the answer to that question made itself known on the second night of the period of non-experience.

I had spent the next day in a state - or non-state - of seeming stillness. Despite the apparent ongoing activity of my mind, nothing really seemed to bother me - my nervous system remained relaxed, as if it had been released of its default sense of contraction. The usual little conflicts and obstacles of family life all unfolded as they usually did; the kids had to be hustled off to school, chores and obligations were dispatched, the kids were brought home from school, dinner was made, bedtime was negotiated. But none of it met with any sense of internal resistance in me. There was no sense, either, of things needing to be any particular way. There was just what seemed to be unfolding, exactly in the way it always did, but *also* very evidently *absolutely Nothing*.

It was evening, and the light was fading outside. My daughters were in their rooms, and I was standing in our living room area, speaking to T., who sat on the couch. It was getting cooler outside, and the window was open. I said a few passing words - I forget what, exactly - stepped over to the window, and closed it.

As soon as I finished this activity, the understanding was suddenly shockingly clear:

Nobody just did that.

Which is to say: *Saying some words and closing the window happened.* But nobody - no real, separate Someone - was *actually inside it.*

It was just *Nothing appearing as something happening.* It was just Life, life-ing.

As this realization appeared, a deeper layer of the separate person "Me" seemed to burn away. With this burning came even more of a sense of emptiness.

But at that moment there also arose the stirrings of a suffering, a pain, that would take many days to start to fully unravel itself.

———

Imagine:

You walk to the window and look out. Beyond is a park. In the wide expanse of green you see a white dog, running.

Naturally you do not feel yourself to *be* that dog. You do not try to *own* the personal experience of the dog as it runs through the park, chasing after a butterfly.

You see it as part of the scene, as one with the view. A streak of life moving amongst life. Its story is not *your* story; it is simply just unfolding as the day unfolds, there in the window.

What if the sense of *yourself* became like this?

———

The jewel turns in the light -

Nothing is *This*. Life unfolding, "life-ing".

Blindly. Timelessly. Spacelessly. Unbounded, unknown, absolutely free and absolutely whole (Because how could No-thing possibly *need* anything?)

Somehow, a pattern apparently arises in Life. A structure *in* Nothing, *made* of Nothing (that's why it's "apparent"). "How" it arises is unknown and unknowable, a paradox, because it both does and doesn't *actually* arise.

Perhaps for the sake of argument we could say it is like a whirlpool forming in a river, or an alteration within a single energy field. This pattern *is the sense of a Someone*. An identity, that feels itself to be *separate* from everything outside it.

And as soon as that sense of a Someone is apparently there, there is a Big Bang. The *real* Big Bang, you could say. *Everything* happens - *happening* happens - simultaneously:

Time is born *for Someone*.

Space is born *for Someone*.

The World is born *for Someone*.

Others are born *for Someone*.

Experience is born *for Someone*.

28

A sense of *ownership* appears: "This life is *mine*. This is *my experience*. I have it, I know it, I understand it. I make choices which affect it. I enjoy it, I wrestle with it, I love it, I hate it. I win, I lose, I seek, I find, I seek again."

But this pattern - this sense of Someone being there - *does not really exist*. All it ever really was, or ever *could* be, is boundless, formless Nothing. It is simply *Nothing seeming to be Someone*. It is only with the apparent appearance of that sense of Someone that a whole *Universe of Somethings and Someones* appear, to be known and understood.

Perhaps you could say there is only *one illusion*, from which all others flow: the sense of "Me".

———

when that evening i rose to
close the window and
spoke some passing phrase

the likes of which i might say
it was not an inside who
tipped the latch or moved

its lips between the
greying beard
it was a pattern only

that lighted danced of its
own accord
as you dance too

not here not inside
reach out as dusk comes and
our house turns orange

and take
this hand
these words

which no one
ever said

iii.

See how this pattern is like a ring, a sealed loop?

Once the *sense of a Someone* seemingly appears, *it* "loses" *Nothing*.

It can never *touch* Nothing. It can never *understand* or *experience* Nothing (which is to say, *what it really is*).

The sense of a Someone can't *attain* Nothing, or *do* Nothing, or *find* Nothing. It can't even *awaken to* Nothing, or *return to* Nothing, or "thin out" or "dissolve" or "fall away" or "collapse into" Nothing - not *really*.

It can't "do" any of this because it is the *very nature of the sense of a Someone to be blind to what it truly is.*

Which is to say, Nothing, happening.

———

Again - the sense of a Someone can't *attain* Nothing, or *do* Nothing, or *find* Nothing. It can't *awaken to* Nothing, or *return to* Nothing, or "thin out" or "dissolve" or "fall away" or "collapse into" Nothing - not *really*.

It can't "do" any of this because *it is Nothing already*.

Your sense of a Someone - of "Me" - has *never* really been there.

There was never anyone there to win or lose anything.

There was never anything that could be won, or lost.

There was never anything to be done.

---

iv.

To say more about the suffering that seemed to rise in me in the days following the "window incident", I also have to speak about *bodies*, and I have to speak about *death*.

———

The sense of Someone - this pattern that feels itself to be "Me" - arises in an apparent body. I say "apparent" because the body, like everything else, is really only Nothing-appearing-as-a-body.

The "Me pattern" is *deep down*. Some who speak about these things say that the sense of a Someone or the Me pattern is "purely energetic", which is another way of trying to express that the Me pattern is *not a thought or a concept*, it is *not an emotion*, it is *not a sensation*, even.

You might say it is the *grounds of possibility* for personal thought, emotion, and sensation.

It is the little whirlpool in the river that *appears* to be a solid form, but is in fact only the water of the river. It is a *deep structure* - the structure of a Someone.

Once this sense of Someone is seemingly in place, the whole story of the person simultaneously begins. Our history, our thoughts and emotions, our suffering and joy, our traumas and triumphs, all the experiences of our identity - all of it spontaneously seems to unfold in time.

"Me", and the whole universe of its experience, feels completely, viscerally, profoundly *real* to the sense of Someone. Our sensations, our emotions, our thoughts, our physical reality in a physical world, with which we interact - *it all feels so completely real.*

And as the real-feeling Someone seems to get older in time, all these real-feeling experiences are layered into our apparent muscles and tendons and fascias and nervous systems.

The sense of a Someone entangles itself with the body.

———

During my period of non-experience, thoughts and emotions came up regularly in my body. Sometimes very *loud* thoughts and very *intense* emotions came up.

But when there is no convincing sense of a separate Someone, when there is no one there, *there is nothing to which these thoughts and emotions can stick.* There is nothing convincingly there to *identify* with them, to own them, to claim them as "mine".

There is just an apparent body, thinking and feeling.

But this also means that there is nothing there to *resist* the thoughts and emotions, either. There is no sense of Someone to judge them, or question them, or seek to avoid them. So you could say the thoughts and emotions are *free* - free to express themselves completely, in their entirety.

For a sense of a Someone that is "thinning-out", this can feel incredibly intense. It can feel like painful suffering.

For me, what followed the "window incident" was a period of disorientation and pain. There was no longer a convincing sense of separation, but all the patterns of thoughts and emotions that had been layered down into my mind and body were still playing themselves out.

My deepest programming, which has always coalesced around a sense of lack - my anxieties and fears and insecurities - would in some ways rise up *more intensely than ever.*

But now *there was nowhere for them to go anymore,* no real-feeling-Someone to meet them. And so they were completely free to overcome my body and then disperse, like a powerful storm raging and finally passing. These storms shook me many times during those days.

---

it can be a savage thing
this rising of life
in the chest the throat

a flock of birds
wildly twisting
flashing

vacuoles
forming then
reforming again

where is it they
want to go
with no roost

or place to claw or
shore up their
din and clatter

their triumph
loss it is all so
felt

but still

wings beat beat
until they
are just the sky

V.

Another spectre that appeared during this period was *grief.* That's not surprising. Because to speak of Nothing is in the same breath to speak of Death.

The sense of a Someone is a sealed loop. It cannot touch the Nothing that is its true nature, *because its very definition is knowing itself as separate.*

You could say that the only way for Someone to "escape" the loop is to die. The ending of the sense of Someone *is* death.

The death of Time *for Someone.*

The death of Space *for Someone.*

The death of The World *for Someone.*

The death of Others *for Someone.*

The death of Experience *for Someone.*

The sense of a Someone - the "Me" - can never understand or achieve or know Nothing, because it can never understand or achieve or know Death.

———

Which is to say, when it dies, the very thing that *could* understand or achieve or know anything is simply no longer there.

———

When the sense of a Someone is "still thinning", you might say the person is "still dying". And this process can seem to bring about a painful sense of grief.

The first inkling of this was when I started to be concerned about my work.

How can I do my job, I thought, *now that it seems completely evident that there is Nothing happening and No one here?*

How can No one do anything at all? If there is no personal need, no personal wanting anymore, will my work just cease to happen now? Will I lose all attachment to my writing?

Nervous, I sat down in my office at my computer, and opened up the piece I was working on.

A strong sense rose up: *The body knows what to do.*

I typed, and *writing simply started happening.* The structure of "me" was still apparently present, like a program that was still running, or a logic that was playing itself out, inside an apparent body. Except that now there didn't feel like there was anything *identifying* with that program. There was nothing really *in* there, calling it "Me" or "Mine". There was nothing *owning* it, nothing *driving* it, or *claiming* it.

This person was just doing what this person apparently does, *without a centre.* Just part of Life, apparently life-ing.

And so I wrote that day, and the work got done.

———

In fact there was a sense of *efficiency* to it now. A kind of *frictionless-ness*. I'm not sure if I can say the work was *better* than before - the question of better or worse seems moot. It's more that it did not seem necessary or even possible to *worry* too much about the work. There was no real sense of *resistance* to it, or *mania* about it either. When such thoughts or feelings - worry or mania, say - seemed to come up, there was an immediate recognition that these thoughts and feelings were not coming up *for* anybody. And so they dissolved away quite quickly. After all, *what else could they do?*

The weather passed. What had to be done was simply done.

It seemed amazing to me at first, this sense of efficiency. So much that had seemed to plague the Someone, so many anxieties and resistances, were now just *not sticking*.

Then over those next several days the amazement became quieter - still there, but calmer, more ordinary-feeling. The sense of simple efficiency seemed less remarkable. It seemed *natural*. Constantly joyful, constantly awe-inspiring - and completely natural.

Imagine that one apparent day, the deep Me pattern starts to fall apart, to burn away, until it is simply no longer there.

The thoughts, the emotions, the experiences of the Someone *do not vanish.*

They just don't belong to Someone anymore.

The world of things and others, *does not vanish.*

The world just doesn't belong to Someone anymore.

Everything that apparently happens *can still happen,* as seemingly ordinary and everyday as before. *It just doesn't belong to Someone anymore.*

Instead, it is seen to be only what it always ever was: *just Life.*

Nothing, happening.

———

But over time it became clear that a sense of concern over work was just the first bloom of this time of apparent suffering. During the next days, there were much deeper aspects of the feeling of grief that started to reveal themselves.

I was standing in the shower one evening. The warm water sluiced down over me, and I gazed at the wall of the glass shower enclosure. On the misted surface, hundreds of dark rivulets worked their way down blindly, in fits and starts.

My sense of Self was burning away.

I saw the people I love - my daughters, my wife, my family. My friends, old and new. And I felt with terrible conviction that *I was leaving them all behind.*

I was suddenly far, far away - a cosmos away - from everyone I cared so deeply about. How could any of them ever understand this, or join me? How could they be with me, here, in this Emptiness?

When I looked into my children's eyes, it would not be "Me" any longer. It would be Nothing. And *they* would be Nothing, too.

Grief rose in me like a terrible crashing wave. Its churning darkness flowed upwards. I started to cry - quietly, so that no family member could hear me.

I felt absolutely uprooted. It was as if I had been going through my days just as I always had been, and then suddenly I had glanced down and seen a vast and formless void beneath me.

Everything that I had taken for granted, had known and believed, was dissolving. "I" the person was going away. What was left of him, standing there alone under the running water, was trying to shore up the ruins, scrabbling in vain to hold on to *Something*.

I was confronting my own death.

I couldn't bear it any longer. I had to speak to T. about all of this. I had to reach out across the Emptiness to her, in fear, and grief; in need, and love.

I finally shared with her as we lay in bed that night, turning my head on my pillow to look her in the eyes. I did my best to explain what had been happening since I had gone up to the top of the hill a week or so ago. I told her how I felt afraid and devastated, how I felt that I was leaving her and our children behind, to depart for... who knows where?

The end of me. Death. *Nothing*.

T. didn't seem shaken - if she was, she didn't betray it. She stroked my arm. She said that, whatever I was going through, what *she* felt in that moment was a sense of safety. She said that she had noticed a seemingly unshakeable good humour in me these past few days, and that was about it. She said that she was there for me - that she and our daughters were not going anywhere. Whatever difficulties came our way, we'd be OK.

It was not so much her words that were so healing, but the sense that what I had told her had not, in fact, pushed her away from me. It seemed to be the opposite; I felt closer to her. The grief that was working in me started to pass through my body.

The jewel turned, and another facet caught the light:

Nothing is *radically intimate*.

It is *absolutely close*. Closer than close.

Nothing can ever be outside of Nothing.

Nothing *already includes Everything*; without judgement, without preference, without hesitation or distinctions.

How can those I love *ever* be apart from me?

We were never really separate.

We were always already included.

———

vi.

Here's the ultimate and most outrageous, as well the quietest and most unremarkable, joke: When the sense of a person dies, it is seen that *there was never anyone alive to begin with.*

No one ever truly dies, because no one was ever truly born.

To speak of Nothing, then, is to speak of Death only *in a sense.*

———————

Which is to say, to speak of Nothing is also to speak of *Love*.

———————

How could we *not* call this Love?

Nothing includes everything. Nothing is left out of Nothing. Nothing is rejected from Nothing. Nothing is resisted by Nothing.

Nothing does not want, or need, or seek to *change* anything. What would there *be* for Nothing - for *This*, for *Life* - to want, or need, or seek to change? What *could* there be?

In this sense, you could say Nothing is *Unconditional* Love.

It is Unconditional Completeness. Unconditional Acceptance. Unconditional Freedom.

It draws absolutely no lines.

Even the feeling of the *lack* of Nothing - even our confusion, our frustrations, our suffering, our endless searching - is *already included in Nothing*.

How could we *not* call this Love?

———

We feel as separate Someones that we are constantly looking for Love. That it is a treasure that eludes us, over and over again. All we ever really want is acceptance and connection. From our partners, our parents, our friends, our family members. We crave it from strangers, from the world at large. And even when we feel we have it, we desperately fear its loss.

But what the separate person *by definition cannot see* is that all it really is, and ever was, *is Love.*

After the death of the person, there is only Unconditional Love, *for no one.*

Love which never died, because it was never even born.

———

your face in the winter
morning blue grey
bedroom barely there
but loved
a whole universe

of memory and wanting
with the black silk
sleep mask ruched up

on your forehead
comical and sly-seeming
puffed and sleep-eyed
almost disappearing
in the pre-dawn shadow

and yet when the light
falls in cool and
slanting

then
you are not
more known

as nothing and no one
is more known
than this

About ten days into my period of non-experience I went for a walk around the neighbourhood with a good friend. Apart from T., during that time C. was the only other person I spoke to about what seemed to be (not-)happening to me. C. and I have shared a lot of experiences with each other, some of them pretty outlandish, but I wasn't sure how he would interpret what I told him as we walked the afternoon sidewalks. What can a person *make* of such a message: "*There's Nothing happening! There's No one here!*"

On the surface at least, he met me with his usual easy-to-laugh good cheer and curiosity. Just as it had been with T., his acceptance was a relief. I consider myself very lucky that I had at least two people close to me at that time who were willing to react this way to what I was saying to them.

Near where I live is the campus of a college. We walked up through the hot, bosky streets towards it. By the time we got to the baseball field at the edge of the campus I had done the best I could to describe to my friend the (non-)events of the last days. C. took it all in silently as we began to circle down between the sandy pink campus buildings.

"Sounds like being a baby," he said after a while. "You know, before we know what's up or down, or part of us, or not part of us. Before we learn how to speak."

His insight hung in the air between us. It seemed to move in the leaves of the trees. C. was already onto the next thought, the next question, but some greater stillness had settled into my body.

It seemed very clear: *When we are infants, there is only the Unknown.*

In the newborn state, the sense of a separate Someone has not yet emerged. We see the world without the need or the ability to *claim* it. On a simple level, we do not yet have the layers of memory and associations that we call "knowing".

For an infant, you could say all the objects of the world are seen *as they truly are*: absolutely unknown, absolutely unknowable.

How could it not be so? When there is only Life, who could there be separate from anything to *know* anything?

As I walked along with C., I remember gesturing at a parked car at the curb. "That is completely unknown!" I said. I pointed at various objects in the view around us - a palm tree, a mailbox: "So is that, and that!"

I had a strange sense of these objects as both existing and non-existent *at the same time*. The car was both a beat-up silver Toyota, glinting dully in the afternoon sun, *and* no-thing, timeless and spaceless. Everything seemed to dance, without clear boundaries.

I was grinning; it hit us both like a huge, wondrous, absurd joke. My friend started to laugh along with me.

It could be said that Nothing is *both* real and unreal, simultaneously.

Or alternatively, Nothing is neither real, *nor* unreal.

How can this be so? The answer is the only true answer there is:

"Unknown."

———

Life is never known.

There isn't even anything separate to it or in it that can *know it is not known.*

The Unknown goes *all the way down.*

———

When we got back to my house, we poured ourselves some water in the kitchen and went out into the garden. We walked up the hill and sat down in exactly the same spot I had sat over a week earlier. We fell into silence, and for a long time neither of us spoke at all.

When all is Unknown, in the end there is only silence.

What is there that could ever be said?

————

Inside that sense of quiet amazement, I also understood more pointedly the fear I had felt previously, in the first week of the non-experience. That feeling of standing over a bottomless void, of losing all my bearings, of *death*.

For a "Me", there can be absolute terror in the Unknown. In fact you could say that the Unknown is in some ways *unbearable* for the sense of a separate Someone.

The sense of a separate Someone will always want to turn Life into an *idea* or a *concept*. That's just what comes naturally to the sense of a Someone. In a way, it is *all Someone is*; the need to know or understand *something*.

The sense of a Someone wants to *make sense*.

———

You could say that the sense of a Someone is a *meaning-making machine*.

But the Unknown is the *end of meaning*.

The Unknown is the *end of sense*.

There is no meaning. There is no sense.

There is no meaninglessness. There is no nonsense.

There is No-thing.

This is freedom.

It's because the sense of a Someone is a meaning-making machine that there is a temptation to turn Nothing into a *position*.

The sense of a separate Someone may hear "All is Nothing" and think: "Oh, I *get it*! All there is is Nothing, so I will *keep that in mind*. I'll behave in a way that aligns with that knowledge."

They might try to deploy various strategies to do this. They might remind themselves at various moments: "Nothing is happening, there's no one really here." This might feel soothing to a Someone, or it might equally feel frustrating - especially if reminding themself that "Nothing is happening and no one is here" *ultimately fails to make anything better for them.*

Or they might try to *practice detachment*. They might decide that being emotionally unattached to events that transpire in their lives is the appropriate course of action, given that the nature of everything is Nothing.

A kind of *nihilism* might even grow inside the mind of a separate Someone. An attitude of "What's the point? Nothing's really happening anyway." The Someone might think that all the suffering and injustices they see in the world around them are *inevitable*, or *meaningless*, or "*just an illusion*" - so the appropriate attitude is apathy, non-participation, and also perhaps a kind of disdain for any other Someones who might think otherwise.

But all of this is just to *take Nothing as a concept.* It's to (sometimes subtly) see Nothing as being *for someone.* It's to remain always and inevitably inside the sealed loop of separation.

———

Practicing detachment can never touch Nothing.

Seeing everything as meaningless can never touch Nothing.

Believing everything is illusionary can never touch Nothing.

Because Everything is always already Nothing, for no one.

---

life said

take an object any
object here this
candle holder

raise it in your
palm to see
brought home

from school by
your daughter
diwali eve

happy little thing
round and squat
a spindle

cut through
dusted with glitter
green and blue

pick out the black
waxed-in wick
with a fingernail

and life said

here
there is no story
no name no

school no
india no
journey no

brush to dust
the glitter no
need

for illumination
no fingernail no
daughter

only itself
ablaze
unknown

This brings me to the end of a story that has no end, because it never had a beginning.

About two weeks after I had sat alone at the top of my garden, a few days after I had sat there again with C., the sense of a Someone seemed to return. It's hard for me to recall whether it happened over the course of a few days or suddenly, overnight. But I know that one day I woke up, and the sense of Emptiness - the absence of a sense of a Someone - had apparently gone. I was "Me" again.

The stillness in my nervous system had been replaced with the usual low-level tension. My familiar wants and needs, my anxieties and frustrations and reactivities, were all right there, present and correct.

Nothing had become a thought, a *memory*.

———

For some days, I reeled from the change. I asked myself: "Why should this have happened? Why did "I" come back?" For a while I felt a sharp sadness, the beginnings of a depression creeping over me.

But most of all I felt *confusion*. It was bewildering. What was the *meaning* of all this?

Then something interesting happened. Quite swiftly after "I" returned, I felt that I had no choice but to accept whatever it was that had happened, and was happening now. Over the following few weeks, I *let it go*. Once I did that, the sadness retreated almost immediately.

When I consider this, I think that it is possible that the sense of a separate Someone, though clearly present again, has become just a little *thinner* than it was before. As time has passed, I have begun to see this residual "thinness" of the sense of separation as a subtle, underlying *lack of conviction in the story of "Me"*. I live my life just as I always have - as a father, a husband, a writer. But somehow the *definitiveness* of experience, the *certainty* in the Someone and its world - all of it seems *less convincing*.

I can say that's where I'm "at" now, here at the moment of writing these words. Perhaps it is *because* the sense of a separate Someone has seemingly returned that I have been drawn to communicate anything about it at all. I'm open to the notion that the desires of "Me" are mixed up with the seemingly spontaneous nature of coming to write this. As I said at the start, take these words only in the spirit in which they are written: as ambassadors of imprecision and uncertainty, as acknowledgements of their own untruth, unable ever to touch the Nothing which is their source, their home, and their nature.

———————

Think of these words as an *echo*. A distant reverberation of Nothing, bouncing off the walls of a seemingly separate mind "here", and seemingly separate minds "out there".

These days, inside that echo, I hear a question. It's quite persistent, even as I acknowledge its paradoxes. It goes like this:

If all our senses of Someones were to burn away tomorrow, what might change in the world?

———

We are close to speaking of the *use* of Nothing here - which is to "miss" Nothing, to fail to speak of it entirely. The end of the sense of a separate Someone does not necessitate change at all. *Anything* may still appear to happen in the boundlessness of Life. Without a pattern of Me, there are simply no distinctions, no *preferences*, no need for something to be one way or another.

But as I said, you might hear the question as an *echo* - the famous finger pointing at the moon, rather than the moon itself.

In that spirit, let's try to answer this echo-question.

———

I grew up the child of political activists and organizers. My father, who is Indian, and my mother, who is the daughter of a second-generation Russian Jew and a Polish Catholic, spent many years passionately fighting for equality and human rights. Perhaps inevitably, I share my parents' values, and I think often with trepidation about the nature of the society, as well as the planetary conditions, that my daughters will grow into.

Much of the current conflict and suffering within ourselves, and in the world around us, is compelled by a relentless drive for *more*. This drive has defined the colonial-capitalist project which has dominated our human societies for the last few hundred years. It can be seen in the pursuit of endless "progress" and growth.

The drive for more has led to a global system in which the constant need to produce profit and increase stock prices has seemingly disconnected us from our sense of shared humanity. It has contributed to extreme inequality and injustice in our societies. In addition, it has driven us directly into the wall of ecological collapse. Catastrophic climate change is no longer a future threat; it is already happening. As I sit here, we have just experienced the hottest July ever recorded globally.

It's hard to ignore the fact that the endless drive for more *is also the fundamental logic of the sense of a separate Someone.*

On a personal level, in our bodies and minds and hearts, don't we always feel, somehow, somewhere, that things *are not quite right*? Or maybe you could say, *not quite finished*?

For a Someone, there is always *something else* that needs to be known. *More* happiness, *more* fulfillment, *more* experience. Which is to say, for the sense of a Someone there is always something *missing*.

In the story of me, I have experienced this again and again - haven't you? I think: "If I can only get this, I will finally be content. I'll be happy, and at peace."

Let's say I've been fortunate, and I manage to do it - I "get this". *Now* I think: "Ah, that wasn't quite it. If I can only get this *other thing* - *then* I'll be happy."

Many of us reach a point in our lives where it seems very clear that nothing we have spent our time and energy seeking seems to give us quite what we wanted or expected. No achievement or experience or relationship or sensation has succeeded in making us feel "done".

If we are in terrible adversity or pain, even the cessation of that adversity or pain does not seem to give us *lasting* peace and happiness. And yet - or perhaps *and so* - it feels like we have no choice but to keep looking.

Now imagine: if the sense of a separate Someone were to simply end, everywhere, for everybody, what apparent behaviors might end with it?

So much of what leads to the *drive for more* writ large in our society is the desire to *dominate* others. Inherent in this is a sense of *lack* - the sense of something missing that must be gained, by proving one's power over another. Without a sense of separation, where would that desire, and that sense of lack, come from, for example?

Similarly, a capitalistic system is fed by a sense of *wanting*. As subjects formed by this system, we have to *keep wanting something* in order to keep feeding the system. We feed it with our money, fundamentally - though in the media age this often gets reified into our *attention*, our fantasies and desires for something *different*, something *else*.

Without a sense of separation, how much *wanting* could be left? Especially a wanting based on a desire for something-that-is-not-*this*? Without a sense of separation, what would underpin an urgent need to accumulate?

These are all yet more echo-questions.

There is truly no telling what may come, because there is only Nothing, happening.

These pages offer only the suggestion of an impossible possibility - that there *can potentially be* the end of a sense of Someone, which was never really there to begin with.

———

There is absolutely no prescription offered here.

There is no suggestion that *something in particular* - some practice, some action - can be done to "bring about" the end of the sense of Someone.

In a very real sense, these words are useless.

This can be frustrating, even infuriating, for the sense of a Someone. In fact it can seem completely *unacceptable.*

Of course it should be so: how could a meaning-making machine ever really accept absolute meaninglessness?

But something else can sometimes happen too, when a message like this is heard.

A deep sense of *relief.*

I think that relief comes from a letting go, however temporary, of all of the unconscious demands of the sense of a separate Someone, which have also been writ large upon the apparent world around us.

What if there was *truly nothing that could be done* with this?

Nothing that could be sought, or attained, or understood, or practiced, or used by Someone?

What if there was simply no need - no possibility, even - for doing or attaining or using?

What if there was nothing missing? What if there was only the radical, impersonal, unconditional acceptance of whatever appears to be here?

What if you could never be bad, or good? Or wrong, or right? Or a failure, or a success?

What if there was never a "you" to begin with?

What would be left?

———

The jewel turns, catching the light.

In the flash of its turning, for a moment it is seen clearly:

Our suffering is already the Love we look for.

Our failed searching, our broken hearts, our frustrations, our traumas, our violences, our moments of weakness, our longings, our fruitless attempts to attain Enlightenment - all this is *already the Love we look for.*

All there is is This.

All there is is Life.

There could never be anything else.

Nothing, appearing as Everything.

———

For no one at all.

———

when he went into the
temple to talk to
life

it said here is one
who is not
here

even as no one ever
was and nothing ever
either

and he wept with
grief for all he would
now leave behind

and life said there
is no one to grieve and
nothing to grieve for

no one to leave and
nothing to leave
behind

like the golden trail
of a star's descent
might fade

and even too
there is no
now

ACKNOWLEDGEMENTS

There are a number of contemporary people who in various ways speak about the message that is suggested or echoed here. I am indebted to all of them. As I mentioned in the Foreword, it's hard enough to attempt to communicate the paradoxes of Nothing, let alone without the aid of those who have beautifully communicated them before me, and continue to do so now. Among those, I would like to mention Rupert Spira; Bernardo Kastrup; Adyashanti; Swami Sarvapriyananda of the Vedanta Society of New York; Tony Parsons; Jim Newman; Andreas Müller; Mei Long.

The Heart Sutra echoes always with this message, as do the *Upanishads* and the *Tao-te Ching*. For a more thorough bibliography than I could ever compile, I recommend *Perfect Brilliant Stillness* by David Carse (Paragate Publishing, 2005).

Suzanne Chang was immensely helpful to me, and I thank her deeply for our conversations.

My thanks to Kelly Karczewski for her enthusiasm and excellent suggestions.

I am forever grateful to Charles Day for his comradeship and his early championing of this text.

For his insight and support, thanks to Michael Gellert.

Finally my profoundest thanks to my wife and family, with whom I am one.

To hear more from the author visit:
www.as-is-press.com